AF244817

8th House Publishing
Montreal, Canada

Copyright © 8th House Publishing 2015
First Edition

Published worldwide by 8th House Publishing.
Front Cover Design by 8th House Publishing

Designed by 8th House Publishing.
www.8thHousePublishing.com
Set in Adobe Caslon Pro, Vieira and Raleway.

Library and Archives Canada Cataloguing in Publication

Demaree, Darren C., author
       Not for art nor prayer : a collection of poetry / by Darren
C. Demaree.

ISBN 978-1-926716-35-0 (paperback)

       I. Title.

PS3604.E56N68 2015   811'.6   C2015-906073-7

Not For ART Nor PRAYER

A COLLECTION OF POETRY

By

DARREN C. DEMAREE

8TH HOUSE PUBLISHING

For Emily, every part of her

She is first seen dancing which is a figure
not for art or prayer or the arousal of desire
but for action simply

Robert Hass, from "The Origin of Cities"

POEMS

Emily As A Mango Hitting the Ground

ACKNOWLEDGEMENTS

The following poems first appeared in the journals and magazines below:

Antiphon: *You Should Say*

Birds Piled Loosely: *Emily As I Slowed the Car Down*

Birmingham Arts Journal: *Emily As A Concept*

Blueline: *Adoration #115, Emily As the Length of a Fox*

Brickplight: *Emily As A Brought Apple*

Colorado Review: *Emily As Luminence Deflected*

Convergence: *Emily As the Campfire Gathers the Branch*

Danse Macabre: *Emily As the Cicada's Song Crests*

Decades Review: *Adoration #91, Adoration #92, Adoration #93*

decomp: *Wednesday Morning #152*

Festival of Language: *Emily As By Choice this Time, Emily As the Audacity of Retaliation, Emily As A Ghost Deer*

Fjords Review (Public Poetry Series): *Emily As the Aftermath of A Vibrant Image*

Ikleftiko: *Wednesday Morning #172, Wednesday Morning #173*

(Insert Coin Here) Anthology: *The End of Folk Songs*

Liver of Dixie Anthology: *Without Lamentations*

Louisville Review: *We Did Our Best to Breathe Into It*

Lullwater Review: *Adoration #6*

Lunch Ticket: *A Brief Suspension of All History #2*

ken*again: *Adoration #164, Adoration #165*

Main Street Rag: *Emily As Unfragile*

Midway Journal: *Emily As Sometimes this Comes Close to an Attempt at Alchemy*

Mind(less) Muses: *Adoration #88, Adoration #90*

The New Poet: *Wednesday Morning #19, Wednesday Morning #20, Wednesday Morning #21*

North Dakota Review: *The Narrow Cut, The Tension Between the Concrete and the Ethereal*

Northwind: *Adoration #28, Adoration #30*
On the Rusk: *Wednesday Morning #64, Wednesday Morning #65,*
                                       Wednesday Morning #66
Petals in the Pan Anthology: *The Overcurrent*
Pif: *Emily As Written by Aase Berg*
Prick of the Spindle: *Emily As the Sun Is So Bright the Field Has*
                                   No Context for the Cold
Pyrokinection: *Wednesday Morning #136, Wednesday Morning #138*
Red Fez: *Adoration #100*
Right Hand Pointing: *Adoration #33*
Rust + Moth: *Adoration #131*
Scapegoat Review: *The Younger Poet Asks Questions of Ohio*
Sentinel Literary Quarterly: *Adoration #141*
Shot Glass Journal: *Adoration #147*
Spry: *Adoration #83*
Stirring: *The Ice Will Keep Our Tide at the Ready*
Straight Forward: *Wednesday Morning #88, Wednesday*
                                       Morning #89
Squawk Back: *Adoration #172, Adoration #174*
Subliminal Interiors: *Adoration #192*
Thrush: *Emily As An Uneaten Clementine*
Tiger's Eye: *Adoration #56*
trans lit: *Emily As the Wind Strikes*
Tuscaloosa Runs This Anthology: *Water Always Leave the Knife*
Two Hawks Quarterly: *Emily As A Sugar Horizon, Emily As Erotica*
                                       At the Table
Up the Staircase: *Emily As Later, Jolted from A Dream*
The Writing Disorder: *Adoration #109, Adoration #110, Adoration*
                                       #111
Your Impossible Voice: *Emily As A Mango Hitting the Ground*

Not For
ART
Nor
PRAYER

DARREN C. DEMAREE

ADORATIONS

ADORATION #6

for the couple in the Chipotle parking lot

I have seen sweeter bones tapping
the bulk of our time together
& though I was in a hurry

to get home, eat this burrito
before my family returned
from swimming, it was lovely to

spend those moments lessening my
own loneliness. You gave me pause.
I wish outlandish joy for you.

ADORATION #28

*for Whitey, a family friend and assistant
clubhouse manager for the Cleveland Indians*

You were the first
inheritance
of Ohio I

knew, your short, bent
body, always
in labor, com-

pressed, never beat-
en. When your pride
flexed, a smile.

ADORATION #30

for Anna, my neighbor

The first time you mentioned your breasts
to me it was to tell me they
were gone now, that there were other

parts missing as well, taken from
your body, from waking flesh
that had woken up poorly, sick.

When I tried consolation, you
made a joke. You looked stronger then.
Actual strength is astounding.

ADORATION #33

*for Reuben, who once worked at Steinkeller with
me in Oxford, Ohio*

We are both very pleased that no-
body died in that firetrap bar,
because surely they would have died

listening to us bitch about
women that didn't love us back.
When one loved me back, you arrived

at our wedding like a stomach
that would never be full. Reuben,
I loved your emptiness. It was pure.

ADORATION #56

for Christopher Michel

Here is
the box
I in-

tended
to wrap
for you;

the gift,
though, was
too big.

ADORATION #83

for my grandmother, Gloria

Ninety
broken
pieces

can be
turned in-
to any-

thing you
want. Meld
the truth.

ADORATION #88

for Phil Stutzman

Youth and elsewhere,
we were born on
the gravel of Lamb

Park, the scuttled
bearing of un-
clean dirt, where our

knees first learned blood
would come with each
flight in the field.

ADORATION #90

for the manager at the Krogers

Yes, I saw, in fact I read it
out-loud to my daughter that we
we're not supposed to ride inside

the cart, but with my son sitting
under buckle, we had no choice,
but to chance that she might, at some

point, stand up to reach for pancake
mix. The running and singing was
my fault. We were having such fun.

ADORATION #91

for Mark Yakich

Dry clarity
in the low grass
& always mid-

season, I have
stared at the rust
on my back door

without longing.
The long fire holds
all poses here.

ADORATION #92

for Elizabeth Herbert

Sometimes
there is
one girl

meant to
splinter
your aw-

fullness.
She hates
her role.

ADORATION #93

*for the elderly man at Teejay's Country
Restaurant*

Un-ready to be responding
to any stricken time, I am
imagining for both of us

that our wives have passed on into
nothingness, that we have only
each other and our water cups

accumulating time by over-
flowing. They return and I toast
our good fortune with coffee, cream.

ADORATION #100

for Gretchen Marty

The woman can
be completely
incomplete, but

if she needed
only two steps
to be full-frame,

she would give you
one of them. She
is rain, not pool.

ADORATION #109

for the delivery guy from Jimmy Johns

When anyone says
have a great fuck-
ing day, it makes

you think you can
have a great fuck-
ing day. Plus, now

you have some chips
& a sandwich.
This can be good.

ADORATION #110

for my son

Absent
teeth, now
present,

like gravel
between
two ponds,

I under-
stand
your cry.

ADORATION #111

for Nik De Dominic

I know all of the different
ways to hold gravel in a drive-
way in Ohio, but I think

I learned what to do with those rocks
in Alabama, how to toss
them casually near train tracks

most of the time because you can
only throw a few of them through
windows without dropping your smoke.

ADORATION #115

for Jean Maddocks

Thoughtless balance,
we are able
to walk back through

the once star-burst
lilies we re-
member as good

axle to our wheels
& when we tell
stories, they turn.

ADORATION #131

*for the young couple in the AT&T store on
Henderson Rd.*

I know
for sure
if you

keep each
other's
hands deep

inside
the sweet
grove, fruit!

ADORATION #141

for the only child in the sick waiting room at Dr. Maher's office

I always want to know how they
are doing in the room without
the television, with old toys,

wiped hourly like their noses,
left there with an over-anxious
parent, doing nervous dances

& always staring at the clock.
Today, there was one caped boy fly-
ing, ignoring his mom, the room.

ADORATION #147

for Robert Demaree

Where the war could collect whole selves
& the names of an entire
generation became much more

mythology than the dry grass
that covered their last shelves. Light, dry,
you knew some of the older boys

that returned and never came back,
you told your girl it would have made
sense to die then, but you loved her.

ADORATION #164

*for the oil painting salesman camped out in
Worthington*

Art hatched
like birds
without

real bones,
it takes
a car

racing
past to
see flight.

ADORATION #165

for Dana Levin

Every photo taken re-
moves the shadow, takes the chimney
from above the flower, hides it

back inside the house where eyes hide,
too. I take photos of my kids.
You do the same. It appears all

of the world could be your offspring.
There is comfort in that thought, warmth
& a circle that could be arms.

ADORATION #172

for the server at the Blue Danube

Dim warmth, it takes
comfort food thrown
at your table

& five stories
told for each half
of your sandwich

to lift the day
from the hard cliff,
the steep edges.

ADORATION #174

for the librarian in the cat socks at Whetstone

There are some days when even in
good light, the devourer weighs
against our chests, we move slowly

with a feeling of sick or dark
tidings. The kids feel it before
I do. They move quietly be-

side me as we exit, then we
enter. There! Bright blue feline tails
wrapping up legs. Such good silly!

ADORATION #192

for Claudia Serea

I think you like water that grows,
surrounds heavy cement, makes those
awful statues of those awful

men and makes them play things, drowns them
for ducks to mock. I think your good
water surrounds, never swallows

the awful past, allows the burn
of time to dissolve it. Lovely,
we can't drink your water, not yet.

ALL OF THEM WHOLE

WE DID OUR BEST TO BREATHE INTO IT

Lung punctured, we did our best to breathe
into the sheep's mouth. Emily even covered
the bloody hole from where the metal, shorn
from the fence post first stuck the animal,
stuck deep into the soft, red tissue, now unwilling
to expand the way it should. We did too much
for an animal we witnessed injured from our car,
did too much to bloody our clothes on Route 3,
while family waited for us to eat a holiday meal.
But we needed to save something then, needed
to put our mouths on something desperate,
fighting to survive with righteous intention. We,
yelling about sex, the having it, the not having it
enough, saw the spearing take the shoulder first,
then plunge deeper still, while Emily took the gravel
quickly and we burst from the car in shock.
The animal died before the farmer, the owner,
or the veterinarian could arrive, or pronounce hope
& I with my tongue warm from the expellant
of life looked at my lovely wife, her sweater torn
& I with my tongue, my tears only for the sheep,
asked her to hold me, despite my wavering hands.

WATER ALWAYS LEAVES THE KNIFE

For Tuscaloosa

How the chip
& hammer,
so paused in both,

that we live with the carry
& away
of that sun sum

of what fingers do
when it's char
or the painted red faces

of about, of about
the town. Rats,
lost scorpions,

the full ribs
of such beauty
is blood, is fat, is ship.

WITHOUT LAMENTATIONS

Song of the sudden blood, the dark heat
& fabulous monsters living without fear
that Egan's might, at some point, collapse

into Hell, that nobody would notice, that
the bay of the hounds would fit in without
a pause in a single dart game, because

fuck all man, we're here, we might as well
have a good time with these transcendental
women, all dressed like they knew this drop

was coming. All beautiful, memoir marvels,
we all rushed to arrive, to interrupt
the discovery, the strain and echo

of the knowledge that even if salvation
comes to the place, nobody would give a shit
& these women would still be here, holding

a tallboy, arguing with each other about men
or art or how best to ruin both with a good dress,
meant for summer, that fits with the devil,

depending on the woman and her beliefs.

THE ICE WILL KEEP OUR TIDE AT THE READY

For John McCormick, Yvonne Rutford, and Ryan Vine

A monument to the possibility
that a seven-year soup may be
required to feel the heat of good

action again, I have decided
to perch myself next to Lake Superior,
to cancel flights, slash tires, give

the wind a good shot at me
from all angles. I see how often
the water wants to rise. I see how

so many people can balk at walking
across the this division of animal
& the animal of the water's assault.

Numb with beauty, eventually
I expect to be numbed by caution,
but if we decided to release

two million balloons from the shore-
line, they would be in Canada
before they ever understood the fear

that was driving them north. There!
A roll of the lake's shoulders, a heave
of spirit, a sneaky lick of the large,

black rocks. On second thought,
maybe I will just take a picture
& witness this sequence from Duluth,

where the dominos of the season
will only slightly rattle my belief
that all of that ice will someday find

me in Ohio, will deliver a message
that I really never understood
what it was the particulars

of this ghost spring can really do.
The jewel never chooses the setting.
The energy is mostly spent building

answers to what might happen next
& from almost every angle this great,
heaving body feels like a beautiful threat.

WHAT GOOD HOME

for Erin Elizabeth Smith

If I am ever found
outside of Ohio,
comfortable, functioning

with any real gravitas,
you will have followed
the chicken bones

Erin has scattered on
my path. I could never be
neatened by her world,

but I could be delirious
& I could show that
to you, simply because

her strong coven allows
my sort of magic
to become sustenance.

Between that warmth
& the occasional chicken,
you would find me fat,

caked in happiness,
taking down whole trees
with a venerable work.

THE YOUNGER POET ASKS QUESTIONS OF OHIO

for Andrew Koch

Already posing, un-bloodied,
I was asked by talent, what it was
like to live in Ohio. I was asked

by the next champion if the food
was any good, what the weather
was like, could he get tickets

to a hockey game, were there
enough sheltering hands to carry
him, his love, their pale stones?

He's a good kid. I've looked him up.
He is the next champion, here,
but I get to work him over a bit

before he comes to the bottom
of my ravine to take this home-
made belt. I really like this kid.

He's got good, active blood,
which should keep him warm
during the hard times to come.

A BRIEF SUSPENSION OF ALL HISTORY #2

I have plans
on the thick part
of my hands

& when they flush
with un-tender
flesh, build

like a mountain
risen to escape
my own bones,

you will see
the structures
behind me. All

of them speaking
of my shoulders.
All of them whole

& personal
& held fast
to my own Ohio.

THE NARROW CUT

We lost the silver
of the mirror, lost
the space between

the kitchen wall
& the brutal intervention
of coming winter.

Studded with boiling,
adamant bodies,
refusing to lie down

on the chilled floor
we have left all burners
on high. Bearable,

with wasted gas
& electric we found
room beneath the table,

where the cat's bowl rests
to take the proper toll
of the season

from each other's flanks.

THE TENSION BETWEEN THE CONCRETE AND THE ETHEREAL

Sank the dark, the lines
we've drawn in the air,
the yellow of which

appears only in fading.
Breathless, because more breath
only pushes the printless beach

closer to the dirty echo
we've constructed below.
Heaven or no, who can speak

for anyone? I've climbed
stairs to reach metal cans,
I've fallen down freeing a bird.

THE OVERCURRENT

Too bloomed
to be subtle, the rendering
of this hung light
is one for full, epic display
& hooding of the triumphant
death. It is astonishing
that each collection of passed
nature is one of sadness
to so many people.
A goal has been met. The seed
has been planted, has grown
to be ecstatic
& hallelujah, gave way
to more beauty. Be tender
with the inelegant tissues
of the failing root,
but do not for one moment
doubt the absolute glory
it was given
by your first, bold glances.

YOU SHOULD SAY

Scraped hollow, it was only fruit
you said, as you pointed to the painting,
with no purpose but to return
my eyes to the picture of the pomegranate,
to focus me on the nonhuman world
of the still-life. You said, last night
you packed into boxes, you took the fragments,
the seeds of the fight, buried them
under old records, under sweaters
& other sewn up things. Slice a circle
out of any wall, whether museum or not,
I said, you will find art, you will find rot,
you will find the color of all hidden things.
I said, you should say that you're sorry.
You said, I don't have to do more
than remember where the scissors are,
because scotch tape and cardboard are weak
& our eyesight might be salty, but it's clear.

THE END OF FOLK SONGS

All night the wind
hasn't mattered,
the moon has risen

without consequence
& I, having given
up the idea of making

love with anyone
at all, have kept the glow
of partially-planned

consciousness humming.
In these moments,
it takes only one wash

of the face to return
from the digital land
of garish warriors

& sports teams
that never perform
like this in real life,

but why would I wait
for a train that will never
arrive anywhere near

my house? Just then,
a sound, a knock,
a chance that the noise

could be an engine
for a better evening
than this. Shit!

I forgot my wallet
in the basement, I'll be
right back with your tip.

WEDNESDAY MORNINGS

WEDNESDAY MORNING #19

Muddy, my un-innocence
is without honey, without

a buzz. Sober, I claim
these sounds as nectar.

WEDNESDAY MORNING #20

I want the crumbling
meat of stars

to roll my hands in,
show you hope exists.

Darren C. Demaree

WEDNESDAY MORNING #21

How righteous
it feels
to linger
in the ecstatic?

More cloud
than lightning,
you should
endeavor.

WEDNESDAY MORNING #34

I am not lonely
on top of the world.

There is great company
in the distance.

WEDNESDAY MORNING #35

Soft-hearted, beating
hard,

I must look tough
wanting

this gentleness
to be everywhere.

My rebellion opens.

WEDNESDAY MORNING #36

I saw the candles first.
There was no one else.
I must have lit them
                    yesterday.

WEDNESDAY MORNING #64

Children on my chest,
today is already mine,

they know it
to be their own victory.

WEDNESDAY MORNING #65

Empty parking lot,
you are sea

& fruit, everything
born dreaming

of absolute freedom
without consequence.

WEDNESDAY MORNING #66

The butcher's knife
is a wide world,

I say out loud.
My children,

graciously nod,
impressed.

WEDNESDAY MORNING #88

Cannonball, I have neither
the rippling belly, nor the carnival
to make you a profitable angel.

WEDNESDAY MORNING #89

I did not
mind
losing

my dream,
it was nice,
simple.

I knew
I was
sleeping.

WEDNESDAY MORNING #136

The energy
of uncoiling

is brief,
but early

morning
all I need

is that much
belief.

WEDNESDAY MORNING #138

The wound
is collection,
un-swiveled,

repeatedly
struck skin,
that knows

better is more
than a pivot.

WEDNESDAY MORNING #152

Hours before
lunch
& my beard

is stained
by milkshake.
I have

only spent
fireworks
today.

WEDNESDAY MORNING #172

I wanted
to write poems
about absence,

but I had
no reason
why I should.

WEDNESDAY MORNING #173

Deep, welcoming
thunder,

release everything!
I want the rain,

the light, the energy
& what follows.

EMILY AS A MANGO HITTING THE GROUND

EMILY AS LUMINENCE DEFLECTED

The first letter that magnificence wrote
was in deference

to the lord. The second letter
that magnificence wrote was about a tide

of angels overwhelming the shores,
confronting the sun. The third letter

was a confession
that magnificence believed only in the heat

of other magnificence
& the army of heavens, General

& Co., seemed to only carry individuals
on the sand, one at a time, driving

them mad with the thought that they
might not be alone. The fourth letter

magnificence wrote was more of a song,
that buried the burden of proof

inside of her glorious, malleable intention
to be weak beauty, but beauty all the same.

EMILY AS THE CAMPFIRE GATHERS THE BRANCH

Swimming deeper into the night, the softness
left the scene when we were able to form a name
for the fire, when we were able to dip the flowers

from the garden into the fire without cause or care,
we knew then that all we had done was create
hunger and give hunger a name we could say

with smoke in our eyes. Turning away, cowardly,
I dragged my hand across my face to wipe the chase
of the tendrils to my sweater. Emily added more

wood the to the flame. She changed the shape
of the mouth in the pit, flushed the sparks towards
the cuff of our pants. She loves doing that shit.

EMILY AS THE WIND STRIKES

If you see an apple
orchard flying past
your house, that is

Emily showing
no pity to nature
& if you see me,

holding the seeds
of a dozen apples,
it is an apology

for I knew not
what it meant
to blitz the world

with this intent
(to abstract, to re-
assemble a love

for art's purpose)
& when I lost
control of Emily,

the pieces of her,
I did not know
you would find out.

EMILY AS BY CHOICE THIS TIME

Delivered near the sweetgum
that grew without being planted
behind our cinder-block garage,

Emily and I found our aging
cat digging towards the root system,
inspired to learn the color

of such a deepening plant. Two
hands, with bones almost as light
as wings, I joined in to escalate

the curious nature of the situation.
Emily sat on the bench next to
the fire pit and lit the first cigarette

she had lit in years. I asked her
about her actions, and she
asked me about my own. The cat

wandered away without answers.
For a while we talked about nothing,
but where we could replant the tree,

where it could be seen and continue
to grow to be seen. She tossed the butt
onto the bricks and walked away.

We agreed later on, after a hot afternoon
in the dirt, that a third child could be
something we would both really want.

EMILY AS THE LENGTH OF A FOX

I haven't the time
to find a bluff
to overlook an expanse
& understand
Emily.
I am in the densest part
of the woods with her
now, the deep
where you touch
everything at once
& believe in the small
bits of your flesh
that you can predict
the next tree that will move
& the next animal
that will eat the next animal
& that shared breath
of meat
is as indelicate
as closeness can be.

EMILY AS LATER, JOLTED FROM A DREAM

There are giant bones
in Emily's dreams
& they hold up the giant legs
of giant people
& when they walk, each step
takes away the sharp-edged light
of Ohio
& each direction they chose
becomes nostalgic
for the simple foliage
& that is what Emily does
in her dreams, she plants
cheap bushes where giants
have walked.
That's beautiful
I tell her all of the time
& she says that she really wishes
that the giants, with their legs
that can ruin everything
didn't, each of them, have my face.
No matter, I tell her all of the time,
I think it's really lovely,
how you frame our world
& have a passion
to tend to everything
that I have tried to destroy.

EMILY AS WRITTEN BY AASE BERG

I believe in the relative
success of the synapse
& if Emily wants to be

part of that crackling,
she will pop to join
me past the dimensional

leanings of her present.
If Emily is entirely real
& here, we will see her.

EMILY AS I SLOWED THE CAR DOWN

I wanted to reach the forest
before the morning
took the danger away
& the light found us
being dangerous with each other
on land that several people claimed to own
& nobody has wired up yet
& Emily wanted the road
to be a path we worked our way through.
I was beating the weather
& I was beating the sun
& she saw me tallying all of that
& with her mouth
she made the marble clear
& we never reached the forest,
until she wanted us to.
We made breakfast together,
in the slight rain that tagged along
with us. We hiked closer to the clouds.
We talked for a long time
about what we could see in this light.

EMILY AS A CONCEPT

Old facts, flesh
favorite of mine,
Emily is fictional

& un-fictional, she
is the hum
of my hungers

& for a woman
of her height, I've
extended her

name into myth,
the elegance
of which, lyric

& hypnotic,
overwhelms
the folding birds.

EMILY AS THE SUN IS SO BRIGHT THE FIELD HAS NO CONTEXT FOR THE COLD

There is a distance from us
to the cut bank, but the warmth,
or absence of the warmth
never varies, never layers jealousy
between the land, the man,
the woman he loves who stares

at the sun without regard for her
eyesight, what that narrowing
black can mean. We are dressed
for a warmer world. We believed
that bright sun meant something.
Legs over the erosion of the field,

we have sat here all morning
hoping more land would develop
so we could lay down in the light.
But that is not what happens here.
No matter what the scene might
look like from Route 36, we are

not moving because we are waiting,
not because we are frozen, or afraid
we will fall into the shallow water
beneath us, we are waiting for eyes
that can decipher all of the things
the steam pouring out of our mouths

might mean. Good money down,
we have nothing to say about Ohio,
as we knew this might happen,
that the small strips of land
might one day mean something more
to us because of the distance

between each other, our warm bodies.

EMILY AS THE AFTERMATH OF A VIBRANT IMAGE

The end of art,
when your stare
takes the simple

physics of sight
& the biology
of a wanting eye,

an eye that lacks
craft, lacks fiction
& simply gives

up the moisture
of the moment.
I have stared

at Emily, past
her girlishness
her burst of body,

her womanhood,
her collection
of outstanding

empathies, I
have framed her
& lost completely

my sight for her.
To begin again,
I must ask her,

this time, for
permission to try
& love her

without motive.

EMILY AS A SUGAR HORIZON

Bring the moon closer, darling,
I like to press my face to you,
your sky, and on my toes, stretched

to the limits of the veins in my neck,
I feel nothing but the cooling air
picking apart my hair, searching

for something sweet. There was
a great temptation to lick the dark
horizon as it changed to reflect

the scattering of your engagement
with the evening. I have a vivid
memory of the night ending

with my tepid body, giving credit
to your resistance. I remember
you fell asleep naked, without review.

EMILY AS EROTICA AT THE TABLE

Drop that napkin, let's let the melting cheese
be a call to arms, the tomato bread bowls
brimming with promise of more bread under-

neath the soup, and your arms Emily, tender
with speed as you desperately try not to spill
your favorite meal on the baby's developing

bald spot. I will ignore the older child, the girl,
if you can reach across the table, if you can wipe
the red promises from my cheek, as astray

with my intentions, I have made a mess with
the tools you have given me to work with tonight.

EMILY AS UNFRAGILE

We named the bigger parts
first; sex, love, marriage,
an un-crooked family crest.

We put fine titles on everything,
but the skeleton, the bones
of which we never named,

the bones we had named for us
as a gift, they were alarming
with strength. I have been shoved

to the ground by my wife
& nothing was broken. She has
driven stakes into my appendages

& yet I am able to hold our children
with actual strength. This
has no name either, but it

should be a religion. In my own
weak heart, it is a religion
with no hidden power source.

EMILY AS A MANGO HITTING THE GROUND

If this were an orchard
how lovely it would be,

if Emily fell from a tree
as the mangos fall, roll

to the will of the root's
gradient. In Ohio, though

we don't grow any mango
& such a fall bruises deeply

what we had first hoped
would be a light pat

from the dirt. Origin
of my fruit, I am sorry,

I did my best to imagine
a way for you to be unscathed

or cradled in good context.
I simply failed to catch you.

EMILY AS SOMETIMES THIS COMES CLOSE TO AN ATTEMPT AT ALCHEMY

Like there might not be a room
beneath the roof that is Emily,
I have done things, they would be

horrible things if they were not
done in the name of Emily?
Yes. There is an incredible

science to relationships, sacrifice
& sacrifice. Is it still a room
if it is devoured by reactions?

Yes. The smoke can be the whole
thing. You can be blinded
& blinding in one supreme action.

EMILY AS IT MATTERS IF THIS IS A FOREST OR A SHIP

After we brush all the bones, pick rocks
that we can shape into vocal cords, sharp
rocks that we can clear thick teases with,

daggers used to build the murmuring
into a mountain that can shine brightly
without fire in the sky. It doesn't matter

if our flesh is a language, but it does
matter what we used our flesh to construct.
If we hollow the scene, we will need wind.

EMILY AS AN UNEATEN CLEMENTINE

The speed of motion
that never touches you
is a bad, bad show.

EMILY AS THE CICADA'S SONG CRESTS

That sound, that was never there
before has now always been there
& if that sound is about to fade,
to grind deeper into the ground
of my subconscious, to the place
where I've left my almost children
& my almost arrests, the littered
moments of where I was almost
a monster, will I be able to remember
the lovely things Emily said to me,
when we had to be louder than
a million magic bugs, singing their
only song, without waver? I will
know Emily as the woman next
to me, and I will love her for that.

EMILY AS A BROUGHT APPLE

Harnessed,
tongue to her flanks

we have run through
the sugar cubes

& yet, fire
to fire, we pierce

the skin of the apple,
because it was there

& our mouths were
no where near done

& as process is flow,
our race is done

& the roses,
her wreath, is on me.

Darren C. Demaree

EMILY AS A GHOST DEER

Threat of a threat,
we are so afraid
of the exact moment

of our ending
that we hold company
like we hold brilliance

taken from nature.
We name company,
put it against our chest.

When company leaves
& returns, the approach
is subtle, pale,

a different shade of alive
& here again!
Good company leaves

many times
& returns more often
than they depart.

Blue, against a sky
with many motives,
I know Emily

will always return
in one form
or another.

EMILY AS THE AUDACITY OF RETALIATION

Emily says she's going
to start writing
about me now,

that she finds me
fascinating, that she gets
to watch me a lot

when I'm not focused
on much, other than
writing about her.

She says her stories
won't be too sad,
but my shoulders

tend to shrink
towards the books
on my desk. I think

she believes I am
most impressive
when I stand up

& face her
like there are no cross
roads, only my body

crossing the lawn
with strenuous purpose.
Typing, I suppose,

does very little
to impress a witness
wishing to partner.

Darren C. Demaree

EMILY AS SHE LOSES FOCUS IN A POEM

Unwilling to be a statue
& painted only in the slants
of shadows, Emily has

started to answer questions
at readings about these poems,
about herself in these poems.

She has heard me talk
about them for years
& I couldn't be more

disappointed that she is cribbing
my answers. I wrote these
for a decade, waiting for her

to get pissed, to take ownership
of them, to ask why I told the truth
& why I lied, why I why

& just kept going without asking her.
She likes it now, when she's naked
& a little bit mean in the poems

& she likes people thinking
that part of her is real. I suppose
I've gotten away with it.

ABOUT THE AUTHOR

Darren C. Demaree is from Mount Vernon, Ohio. He is a graduate of The College of Wooster and Miami University. He is the recipient of five Pushcart Prize nominations. Outside of his own poetry, Darren is the founding editor of AltOhio and Ovenbird Poetry, as well the Managing Editor of the Best of the Net Anthology. Currently, he is living and writing in Columbus, Ohio, with his wife and children. *Not for Art nor Prayer* is his fourth collection of poetry.

ALSO OUT THIS SEASON:

ENSEMBLE by Thomas Phillips
4.7 x 7.5 | 148 pages | ISBN 978-1-926716-29-9 (pbk.) | $15.88

Set in Montreal, Ensemble takes us through the throes of existential crises as lives and marriages are overturned by a man's restless yearning.

A philosopher is suddenly forced to face the questions he lectures on when they materialize out of the theoretical and into the practical after he falls for a student in his class. Meanwhile his wife, an accomplished musician is left to deal with the disintegration of their marriage and the new silence that descends upon her life as she dissects her husband's inner workings and confronts the object of his desire. Told in clinical honesty, Ensemble deconstructs love and relationships in the 21st century.

THE MATCHSTICK GIRL by Suzanne Hocking
5. 5 x 8.5 | 90 pages | ISBN 978-1-926716-35-0 (pbk.) | $15.88

YELENA walks the line between cold and poverty. Then for a brief moment fortune shines on her and Yelena catches a glimpse of hopes and unknown joys that she never imagined could have been within her reach. But as soon as it appears, it is taken from her. Obsession takes hold, and as the years pass, she grows to want far more than what the life of a young girl of the streets can offer. Through luck and deceit, she lands a place at the esteemed Smolny Institute for Noble Girls where the young women of the Russian court are taught mathematics, literature and science and where Yelena hopes to light a fire under Russian society.

THE MATCHSTICK GIRL brings LGBT undercurrents to nineteenth-century Russia, as our young protagonist struggles with class differences, schoolgirl relationships and her search for self-empowerment.

ARIELLE QUEEN - Book I - A Knight for a Queen by Michel Levesque
5 x 8. 130 pages, ISBN 978-1-926716-32-9 (pbk.) . $13.88

The best-selling, award-winning fantasy series by Michel Levesque translated into English

"Fat. Plain. Orphaned." The three words Arielle uses to describe herself. But a secret, both frightening and beautiful, will emerge, like a butterfly from its cocoon.

BOOK I - A KNIGHT FOR A QUEEN
Arielle, an insecure teenager discovers on her sixteenth birthday that life is not as she once thought—boring. Suddenly thrust into the middle of a battle between evil and more evil that has been raging for centuries she learns of another world co-existing with ours. Now, Arielle must discover who she truly is before she can understand all that is happening around her. A journey of self-discovery becomes a life-and-death struggle for our heroine as she battles supernatural forces pursuing her and learns about herself, her destiny and the prophecies foretelling her arrival.

TO RUSSIA WITH LOVE by Damian Siqueiros

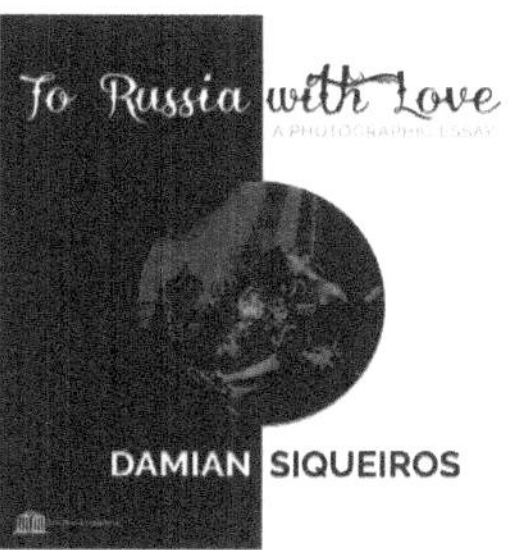

To Russia with Love" is how a group of Montreal artists and collaborators answer the phobias arising out of Russia. This is their stand against the recent wave of bigotry and violence and the realization of the moral imperative to not remain passive in the face of hatred and injustice.

"..exquisitely detailed...." - Phil Tarney, Artists Corner Gallery, Hollywood, California

"Masterful visua. quotations.." - Ivan Savvine, Russian Journalist & Activist

Led by visual artist and photographer Damian Siqueiros, "To Russia with Love" portrays iconic gay and lesbian Russians in all of Siqueiros's usual detail and flare. Along with his collaborators, Mr. Siqueiros is passionate in his belief that fighting hatred with hatred is as nonsensical as trying to extinguish a fire with more fire. There is no condemnation for those perpetrating injustice, instead these portraits serve to remind us of the beauty of love and to validate the couples and the identities of our Russian brothers and sisters in the LGBT community.

A Selection of other 8th House Titles

AS WE REFER TO OUR BODIES by Darren C. Demaree
5 x 8 . 90 pages. ISBN 978-1-926716-16-9 $15.88

Our bodies, our individual and collective bodies, and the separate bodies that together combine to make our systems, ecological, biological, psychological and technological— these are the bodies that we refer to, these are the bodies that Darren C. Demaree has dance for us on the page; nuanced or naked, dissected, desecrated and decorated; these are the bodies that rise and swell to the touch of the poet's pen.

"..a dangerous dreamer..." "unsettling in necessary ways." — Christopher Michel, Author, Editor

THE ENGLISH QABALAH 2nd. Edition, Hardcover
7 x 9.25 | 440 pages | Hard Cover | ISBN 978-1-926716-26-8 | $56.00

A learned exposition by one of the world's leading Qabalists, this book takes the reader through an exploratory journey through the English Alphabet and the mystic and even subconscious roots of our development of language throughout history. A quick survey of the Hebrew Qabalah is presented before embarking the reader upon the discovery of the English Qabalah and the Key to the Roman Script published here for the first time. Disturbingly poetic and irritatingly profound, readers will find a treasure chest of delights to whet their curiosity. - Editor's Review

THE MIDAS TOUCH BY James Cummins & Cameron W. Reed
230 pages. ISBN 978-1-926716-06-0 $23.88

"... a journey into the predatory nature of some of the practices and institutions in the financial industry today . . . ."

Authors James Cummins and Cameron W. Reed take us on an exploratory journey into the predatory nature of some of the practices and institutions in the financial industry today. What seems innocently enough as capitalism and greed gone naturally wild in an environment of deregulation, soon appears as deliberate political manoeuvering and close control on an international scale by agents and institutions operating above the law.

CROSSING TO TADOUSSAC by Frederick E. Bryson
438 pages, 5 x 8, ISBN 978-1-926716-00-8

The FLQ have bombed the Montreal Stock Exchange. The streets are charged and a referendum is called on secession. Frederick E. Bryson captures a defining moment in Canadian history in his latest novel "Crossing to Tadoussac".

KOLKATA DREAMS by K. Gandhar Chakravarty
Colour, Illustrated. ISBN 978-0-9809108-7-2

A work that will transport you across the sea to the idealization and mysticism of the East against the realities of its westernization. Reading and reciting this poetry, you will find that laughter often chokes itself on tears while the book yo-yos between meditation and contemplation.

"A robust, deceptive simplicity hums at the center of this collection..." - YUSEF KOMUNYAKAA, PULITZER PRIZE WINNER FOR POETRY ON "KOLKATA DREAMS"

JUMP THE DEVIL by Richard Rathwell
5 x 8. 146 pages, ISBN 978-1-926716-11-4. $18.88

With Jump the Devil, Richard Rathwell has masterfully interwoven the plots of five seemingly unrelated storylines to create one coherent narrative that spans the globe and works to blend the seemingly mundane with the profound, deftly providing readers the necessary clues to unlocking the story. Transcending borders, cultures, generations, and social mores, Jump the Devil brings to life the notion of the global village as it exists in the 21st Century.

Rathwell's writing is "a fistful of sentences written with the subtlety of a geisha and the terse certainty of stainless steel." - JOHN OLSON, AUTHOR

HYPODROME by Jason Price Everett
148 pages, 5 x 8 ISBN: 978-1-926716-12-1

Jason Price Everett's poetry explodes from the page with the raucous power of industrial machinery and strikes its targets with the rapier's fine point. Honing in on the chaos of the past two decades, Hypodrome charts the growth of today's artist searching for the defining aesthetic of our time. These poems document the plastic, the losses, the frustrations and the triumphs accumulated during the course of an accelerated era set against the backdrop of an ominously beautiful future.

UNFICTIONS by Jason Price Everett
288 pages, 5 x 8. ISBN 978-0-9809108-6-5

Unfictions serves to dramatize the way in which we react to such an information-rich environment in all of its glorious simultaneity - the beginning of a type of 'New Realism' in letters - reflecting faithfully a society so saturated with events and quotations that it can no longer distinguish between them and their relative meanings. "

"...a remarkable achievement and issues a profound challenge to the literary landscape of today." - THE ANTIGONISH REVIEW ON "UNFICTIONS"

MAVOR'S BONES BY ROLLI (CHARLES ANDERSON)
5 x 8 | 121 pages. ISBN 978-1-926716-30-5 (pbk.) | $15.88

"I have been dreaming / those dreams of meaning / that come from the waters / of dreaming deep / like drowned men / to the gold skin / of the ocean"

Company's come. In a ramshackle mansion, meet a family in the same condition—ancient, decayed. There's the brooding Duke, and his riotous brother. There's Grandam, lost in wilds of herself. There's a vicar, a philosopher, an angel, a ghost or two. And somewhere above them all, in a ruined garret...
"By turns delightfully black, singingly lyrical and/or innocently nonsensical. Here is a poet outside the mainstream with his own refreshingly original voice and bone[s] to pick." – Gillian Harding-Russell, author of
I Forgot to Tell You

SEVEN SYRIANS - War Accounts from Syrian Refugees by Diego Cupolo

8 x 8. | 86 pages | Full-Color Photography | ISBN 978-1-926716-26-8 | $18.88
(*$2 of your purchase will go directly to the "A HEART FOR SYRIA" a charity organization supplying humanitarian aid to Syrians displaced by the ongoing war. At least twice a month, a container-load of clothing, blankets and medical supplies leave the port of Montreal to help civilians inside Syria. Find out more and how you can help here.)

"Seven Syrians" captures the stories and struggles of those caught in the middle of the armed conflict currently ravaging Syria. Framed by Diego Cupolo's unerring eye while touring the region, these photographs and first-hand accounts remind us that it is civilians who suffer the brunt of war's atrocities. In a series of humanizing portraits, Diego Cupolo takes us into the lives of those fortunate enough to have survived the conflict decimating their homeland. Forced to flee their homes and families, these men, women and children, teachers, plumbers, engineers, taxi drivers, brothers and sisters no different than ourselves and our neighbours, tell us in their own words of their struggles, triumphs, pains and fortitude and of the monstrosity of war when all of us the world over, seek the same security and opportunities for our children. Read and listen.

THE LOVE SONG OF J. EDGAR HOOVER by Charles Talkoff
5 x 8 . 302 pages. ISBN 978-1-926716-10-7 $23.88

The Ministry of Ambiance, Fluffy-eared Generals, Special Agent Automatic Turpentine, Katzenberg's Super Atomic Piston Fing, Mr. Jellybean and Agency men all vie for your thoughts. Welcome to a post-9/11 paranoid world that would have had Hoover dancing in his closet.

"Talkoff is . . . a serial killer having his way with the entire body of literature, art, and popular culture."
- Jed Birmingham, Author, Editor

SPOILERS by Mark Foss
5.25 x 8, 193 pages. ISBN 978-1-926716-08-4. $18.88

"For now, there is Baldie Fitzgerald. He doesn't know it yet, but he too will be changed."

Sarah. On a wall in a house in Florida she collects postcards and photos from a hundred years ago: Baldie, the young man with one short leg; Ora, the girl with a wandering eye; Jack the chairboy: all three come alive under Sarah's probing gaze.

MAPLE VEDAS by K. Gandhar Chakravarty
Colour with Original Artwork by Tara Chartrand, Chris Dyer, Collen MacIsaac.
6 x 9 . 78 pages. ISBN 978-1-926716-05-3. $18.88

The latest in a long line of scriptures, MAPLE VEDAS explores the voyages of the Gods of India – Vishnu, Shiva, Ganesha, Kali – as they visit the northwestern lands of the globe in the past, the present, and the near future. Peopled with other characters like a prophetic moose, a secretive walrus, and a charming groundhog, the interactions and dialogues of this third millenium testament force you to rethink history, religion, and your place in all of it – wherever you come from.

PLUM STUFF by Rolli (Charles Anderson)
With illustrations by the author. Colour. 5.5 x 8.5. 128 pages. $18.88

Rollick with Rolli through coddled lawns and parlour rooms, sloshing tea with gingercats under bluebird moons and slopping wine with bathing bachelorette hieresses in a world plum-stuffed with all things epicurean and bewitching, from English to Egyptian, the pathologic and the philosophic. By Canada's Charles Anderson (Rolli), recipient of the 2007 John Kenneth Galbraith Literary Award; and winner of the 2008 Commonwealth Short Story Competition.

Visit us online at www.8thHousePublishing.com